MznLnx

Missing Links Exam Preps

Exam Prep for

Intermediate Algebra with Early Functions and Graphing

Lial, Hornsby, McGinnis, 7th Edition

The MznLnx Exam Prep is your link from the texbook and lecture to your exams.
The MznLnx Exam Preps are unauthorized and comprehensive reviews of your textbooks.

All material provided by MznLnx and Rico Publications (c) 2010
Textbook publishers and textbook authors do not particpate in or contribute to these reviews.

MznLnx

Rico
Publications

Exam Prep for Intermediate Algebra with Early Functions and Graphing
7th Edition
Lial, Hornsby, McGinnis

Publisher: Raymond Houge
Assistant Editor: Michael Rouger
Text and Cover Designer: Lisa Buckner
Marketing Manager: Sara Swagger
Project Manager, Editorial Production: Jerry Emerson
Art Director: Vernon Lowerui

Product Manager: Dave Mason
Editorial Assitant: Rachel Guzmanji
Pedagogy: Debra Long
Cover Image: Jim Reed/Getty Images
Text and Cover Printer: City Printing, Inc.
Compositor: Media Mix, Inc.

(c) 2010 Rico Publications
ALL RIGHTS RESERVED. No part of this work
covered by the copyright may be reproduced or
used in any form or by an means--graphic, electronic,
or mechanical, including photocopying, recording,
taping, Web distribution, information storage, and
retrieval systems, or in any other manner--without the
written permission of the publisher.

For more information about our products, contact us at:
Dave.Mason@RicoPublications.com

For permission to use material from this text or
product, submit a request online to:
Dave.Mason@RicoPublications.com

Printed in the United States
ISBN:

Contents

CHAPTER 1
Review of the Real Number System — 1

CHAPTER 2
Linear Equations and Applications — 10

CHAPTER 3
Linear Inequalities and Absolute Value — 12

CHAPTER 4
Graphs, Linear Equations, and Functions — 16

CHAPTER 5
Systems of Linear Equations — 22

CHAPTER 6
Exponents and Polynomials — 26

CHAPTER 7
Rational Expressions — 35

CHAPTER 8
Roots and Radicals — 42

CHAPTER 9
Quadratic Equations, Inequalities, and Graphs — 51

CHAPTER 10
Exponential and Logarithmic Fundions — 58

CHAPTER 11
Nonlinear Fundions, Conic Sections, and Nonlinear Systems — 61

ANSWER KEY — 66

TO THE STUDENT

COMPREHENSIVE

The *MznLnx* Exam Prep series is designed to help you pass your exams. Editors at MznLnx review your textbooks and then prepare these practice exams to help you master the textbook material. Unlike study guides, workbooks, and practice tests provided by the texbook publisher and textbook authors, *MznLnx* gives you **all** of the material in each chapter in exam form, not just samples, so you can be sure to nail your exam.

MECHANICAL

The MznLnx Exam Prep series creates exams that will help you learn the subject matter as well as test you on your understanding. Each question is designed to help you master the concept. Just working through the exams, you gain an understanding of the subject--its a simple mechanical process that produces success.

INTEGRATED STUDY GUIDE AND REVIEW

MznLnx is not just a set of exams designed to test you, its also a comprehensive review of the subject content. Each exam question is also a review of the concept, making sure that you will get the answer correct without having to go to other sources of material. You learn as you go! Its the easiest way to pass an exam.

HUMOR

Studying can be tedious and dry. MznLnx's instructional design includes moderate humor within the exam questions on occassion, to break the tedium and revitalize the brain

Chapter 1. Review of the Real Number System

1. In mathematics, and more specifically set theory, the _____ is the unique set having no (zero) members. Some axiomatic set theories assure that the _____ exists by including an axiom of _____; in other theories, its existence can be deduced. Many possible properties of sets are trivially true for the _____.
   a. Abelian P-root group
   b. AKS primality test
   c. ADE classification
   d. Empty set

2. A _____ is a symbol that stands for a value that may vary; the term usually occurs in opposition to constant, which is a symbol for a non-varying value, i.e. completely fixed or fixed in the context of use. The concepts of constants and variables are fundamental to all modern mathematics, science, engineering, and computer programming.

   Much of the basic theory for which we use variables today, such as school geometry and algebra, was developed thousands of years ago, but the use of symbolic formulae and variables is only several hundreds of years old.

   a. -module
   b. 2-bridge knot
   c. -equivalence
   d. Variable

3. In mathematics, a _____ is a rectangular array of numbers. This way, matrices can record data that depend on multiple parameters. In particular they are used to keep track of the coefficients of multiple linear equations. Matrices are closely connected to linear transformations, which are higher-dimensional analogs of linear functions, i.e., functions of the form f(x) = c · x, where c is a constant. This map corresponds to a _____ with one row and column, with entry c. In addition to a number of elementary, entrywise operations such as _____ addition a key notion is _____ multiplication, which displays a number of features not encountered in numbers; for example, products of matrices depend on the order of the factors, unlike products of real numbers, say, where c · d = d · c for any two numbers c and d.
   a. Heap
   b. Commutativity
   c. Polynomial expression
   d. Matrix

4. The _____ are natural numbers including 0 ' href='/wiki/0_(number)'>0, 1, 2, 3, ...) and their negatives (0, −1, −2, −3, ...). They are numbers that can be written without a fractional or decimal component, and fall within the set {...
   a. Abelian P-root group
   b. ADE classification
   c. AKS primality test
   d. Integers

Chapter 1. Review of the Real Number System

5. In mathematics, a _____ is any number that can be expressed in the form

$$\frac{a}{b}, a, b \in \mathbb{Z}, b \neq 0$$

which says 'a divided by b, given that a and b are integers and b does not equal zero'. Since the denominator b may be equal to 1, every integer is a _____. The set of all rational numbers is denoted $\mathbb{Q}$ (for quotient.)

   a. Number system
   b. Ratio
   c. -equivalence
   d. Rational number

6. In mathematics, the _____ of a real number is its numerical value without regard to its sign. So, for example, 3 is the _____ of both 3 and −3.

The _____ of a number a is denoted by $|a|$.

   a. ADE classification
   b. Absolute value
   c. AKS primality test
   d. Abelian P-root group

7. In geometry, a _____ is a straight curve. When geometry is used to model the real world, lines are used to represent straight objects with negligible width and height. Lines are an idealisation of such objects and have no width or height at all and are usually considered to be infinitely long.
   a. -equivalence
   b. -module
   c. 2-bridge knot
   d. Line

8. In mathematics, an _____ is a complex number whose squared value is a real number less than or equal to zero. The imaginary unit, denoted by i or j, is an example of an _____. If y is a real number, then i·y is an _____, because:

$$(i \cdot y)^2 = i^2 \cdot y^2 = -y^2 \leq 0.$$

Imaginary numbers were defined in 1572 by Rafael Bombelli.

a. AKS primality test
b. Imaginary number
c. ADE classification
d. Abelian P-root group

9. In mathematics, the _____ of a number n is the number that, when added to n, yields zero. The _____ of F is denoted −F.

For example, the _____ of 7 is −7, because 7 + (−7) = 0, and the _____ of −0.3 is 0.3, because −0.3 + 0.3 = 0.

a. Artinian ideal
b. Interior algebra
c. Isomorphism class
d. Additive inverse

10. _____ is the mathematical process of putting things together. The plus sign '+' means that numbers are added together. For example, in the picture on the right, there are 3 + 2 apples--meaning three apples and two other apples--which is the same as five apples, since 3 + 2 = 5.
a. ADE classification
b. Addition
c. AKS primality test
d. Abelian P-root group

11. In its simplest meaning in mathematics and logic, an _____ is an action or procedure which produces a new value from one or more input values. There are two common types of operations: unary and binary. Unary operations involve only one value, such as negation and trigonometric functions.
a. Operation
b. Abelian P-root group
c. ADE classification
d. AKS primality test

12. _____ is one of the four basic arithmetic operations; it is the inverse of addition, meaning that if we start with any number and add any number and then subtract the same number we added, we return to the number we started with. _____ is denoted by a minus sign in infix notation.

Chapter 1. Review of the Real Number System

The traditional names for the parts of the formula

c − b = a

are minuend (c) − subtrahend (b) = difference (a.)

a. 2-bridge knot
b. -module
c. -equivalence
d. Subtraction

13. In mathematics, the complex numbers are an extension of the real numbers obtained by adjoining an imaginary unit, denoted i, which satisfies:

$$i^2 = -1.$$

Every _____ can be written in the form a + bi, where a and b are real numbers called the real part and the imaginary part of the _____, respectively.

Complex numbers are a field, and thus have addition, subtraction, multiplication, and division operations. These operations extend the corresponding operations on real numbers, although with a number of additional elegant and useful properties, e.g., negative real numbers can be obtained by squaring complex (imaginary) numbers.

a. -module
b. 2-bridge knot
c. -equivalence
d. Complex number

14. In mathematics, a _____ or reciprocal for a number x, denoted by $1/x$ or x^{-1}, is a number which when multiplied by x yields the multiplicative identity, 1. The _____ of x is also called the reciprocal of x. The _____ of a fraction a/b is b/a.
a. Multiplicative inverse
b. -equivalence
c. 2-bridge knot
d. -module

15. In mathematics, especially in elementary arithmetic, _____ is an arithmetic operation which is the inverse of multiplication.

Specifically, if c times b equals a, written:

$$c \times b = a$$

where b is not zero, then a divided by b equals c, written:

$$\frac{a}{b} = c$$

For instance,

$$\frac{6}{3} = 2$$

since

$$2 \times 3 = 6.$$

In the above expression, a is called the dividend, b the divisor and c the quotient.

   a. 2-bridge knot
   b. -module
   c. -equivalence
   d. Division

16. In mathematics, a _____ of a number x is any number which, when repeatedly multiplied by itself, eventually yields x:

$$r \times r \times \cdots \times r = x.$$

In terms of exponentiation, r is a _____ of x if

$$r^n = x$$

for some positive integer n. For example, 2 is a _____ of 16 since $2^4 = 2 \times 2 \times 2 \times 2 = 16$.

The number n is called the degree of the _____.

a. Root
b. Rationalisation
c. Cubic function
d. Difference of two squares

17. A _____ is a three-dimensional solid object bounded by six square faces, facets or sides, with three meeting at each vertex. The _____ can also be called a regular hexahedron and is one of the five Platonic solids. It is a special kind of square prism, of rectangular parallelepiped and of trigonal trapezohedron.
   a. Cube
   b. -equivalence
   c. 2-bridge knot
   d. -module

18. In mathematics, the word _____ is a term for any well-formed combination of mathematical symbols. For example,

   $x^2 + 3x - 4$

is an _____, while

   $)x) / 0$

is not, because the parentheses are not balanced and division by zero is undefined.

Being an _____ is a syntactic concept - the meaning of the variables is irrelevant, but different fields have different notions of validity.â€€See formal language for how expressions are constructed, and formal semantics for meaning.

   a. Orthogonal
   b. Arity
   c. Unit ring
   d. Expression

19. In elementary algebra, a _____ is a polynomial with two terms--the sum of two monomials--often bound by parenthesis or brackets when operated upon. It is the simplest kind of polynomial other than monomials.

- The _____ a² - b² can be factored as the product of two other binomials:

    a² - b² = (a + b)(a - b.)

    This is a special case of the more general formula:

    $$a^{n+1} - b^{n+1} = (a-b)\sum_{k=0}^{n} a^k b^{n-k}$$

- The product of a pair of linear binomials (ax + b) and (cx + d) is:

    (ax + b)(cx + d) = acx² + axd + bcx + bd.

- A _____ raised to the nth power, represented as

    (a + b)ⁿ

    can be expanded by means of the _____ theorem or, equivalently, using Pascal's triangle. Taking a simple example, the perfect square _____ (p + q)² can be found by squaring the :first digit, adding twice the product of the first and second digit and finally adding the square of the second digit, to give p² + 2pq + q².

a. Theory of equations
b. Generalized arithmetic progression
c. Content
d. Binomial

20. The _____ of a Lie algebra 𝔤 is a particular ideal of 𝔤.

Let 𝔤 be a Lie algebra. The _____ of 𝔤 is defined as the largest solvable ideal of 𝔤.

a. Class sum
b. Cyclically reduced word
c. Garside element
d. Radical

21. In mathematics, a _____ of a number x is a number r such that r² = x, or, in other words, a number r whose square (the result of multiplying the number by itself) is x.

Every non-negative real number x has a unique non-negative _____, called the principal _____, which is denoted with a radical symbol as $\sqrt{x}$, or, using exponent notation, as x^(1/2). For example, the principal _____ of 9 is 3, denoted $\sqrt{9} = 3$, because 3² = 3 × 3 = 9.

a. -module
b. 2-bridge knot
c. -equivalence
d. Square root

22. In group theory, a branch of mathematics, the term _____ is used in two closely related senses:

- the _____ of a group is its cardinality, i.e. the number of its elements;
- the _____, sometimes period, of an element a of a group is the smallest positive integer m such that a^m = e (where e denotes the identity element of the group, and a^m denotes the product of m copies of a.) If no such m exists, we say that a has infinite _____. All elements of finite groups have finite _____.

We denote the _____ of a group G by ord(G) or $|G|$ and the _____ of an element a by ord(a) or $|a|$.

Example. The symmetric group S_3 has the following multiplication table.

This group has six elements, so ord(S_3) = 6.

a. Artin group
b. Order
c. Outer automorphism group
d. Index calculus algorithm

23. In algebra and computer programming, when a number or expression is both preceded and followed by an operator such as minus or times, a rule is needed to specify which operator should be applied first; this rule is known as a _____, or more informally order of operation. From the earliest use of mathematical notation, multiplication took precedence over addition, whichever side of a number it appeared on. Thus 3 + 4 × 5 = 5 × 4 + 3 = 23.

a. Formal power series
b. Setoid
c. Planar ternary ring
d. Precedence rule

24. In mathematics the _____ of a set which is equipped with the operation of addition is an element which, when added to any element x in the set, yields x. One of the most familiar additive identities is the number 0 from elementary mathematics, but additive identities occur in other mathematical structures where addition is defined, such as in groups and rings.

- The _____ familiar from elementary mathematics is zero, denoted 0. For example,

$5 + 0 = 5 = 0 + 5.$

- In the natural numbers N and all of its supersets (the integers Z, the rational numbers Q, the real numbers R, or the complex numbers C), the _____ is 0. Thus for any one of these numbers n,

$n + 0 = n = 0 + n.$

Let N be a set which is closed under the operation of addition, denoted +. An _____ for N is any element e such that for any element n in N,

$e + n = n = n + e.$

a. External
b. Universal algebra
c. Identity element
d. Additive identity

25. In mathematics, an _____ is a special type of element of a set with respect to a binary operation on that set. It leaves other elements unchanged when combined with them. This is used for groups and related concepts.
    a. Orthogonal
    b. Algebraic K-theory
    c. Isomorphism class
    d. Identity element

26. In mathematics, there are several meanings of _____ depending on the subject.

A _____, usually denoted by ° (the _____ symbol), is a measurement of plane angle, representing $1/360$ of a full rotation. When that angle is with respect to a reference meridian, it indicates a location along a great circle of a sphere, such as Earth , Mars, or the celestial sphere.

a. Degree
b. Relation algebra
c. Median algebra
d. Symmetric difference

Chapter 2. Linear Equations and Applications

1. A _____ is one of the basic shapes of geometry: a polygon with three corners or vertices and three sides or edges which are line segments. A _____ with vertices A, B, and C is denoted ABC.

   In Euclidean geometry any three non-collinear points determine a unique _____ and a unique plane (i.e. a two-dimensional Euclidean space.)

   a. -module
   b. Triangle
   c. -equivalence
   d. 2-bridge knot

2. In geometry and trigonometry, an _____ is the figure formed by two rays sharing a common endpoint, called the vertex of the _____ . The magnitude of the _____ is the 'amount of rotation' that separates the two rays, and can be measured by considering the length of circular arc swept out when one ray is rotated about the vertex to coincide with the other Where there is no possibility of confusion, the term '_____' is used interchangeably for both the geometric configuration itself and for its angular magnitude (which is simply a numerical quantity.)
   a. AKS primality test
   b. ADE classification
   c. Abelian P-root group
   d. Angle

3. The _____ are natural numbers including 0 ' href='/wiki/0_(number)'>0, 1, 2, 3, ...) and their negatives (0, −1, −2, −3, ...). They are numbers that can be written without a fractional or decimal component, and fall within the set {...
   a. ADE classification
   b. Abelian P-root group
   c. AKS primality test
   d. Integers

4. In mathematics, the word _____ is a term for any well-formed combination of mathematical symbols. For example,

   $x^2 + 3x - 4$

   is an _____, while

)x) / 0

   is not, because the parentheses are not balanced and division by zero is undefined.

Being an _____ is a syntactic concept - the meaning of the variables is irrelevant, but different fields have different notions of validity.â€See formal language for how expressions are constructed, and formal semantics for meaning.

a. Arity
b. Unit ring
c. Orthogonal
d. Expression

Chapter 3. Linear Inequalities and Absolute Value

1. In mathematics, the _____ of a real number is its numerical value without regard to its sign. So, for example, 3 is the _____ of both 3 and −3.

   The _____ of a number a is denoted by $|a|$.

   a. AKS primality test
   b. Absolute value
   c. ADE classification
   d. Abelian P-root group

2. In geometry, a _____ is a straight curve. When geometry is used to model the real world, lines are used to represent straight objects with negligible width and height. Lines are an idealisation of such objects and have no width or height at all and are usually considered to be infinitely long.
   a. -module
   b. -equivalence
   c. 2-bridge knot
   d. Line

3. A _____ is a symbol that stands for a value that may vary; the term usually occurs in opposition to constant, which is a symbol for a non-varying value, i.e. completely fixed or fixed in the context of use. The concepts of constants and variables are fundamental to all modern mathematics, science, engineering, and computer programming.

   Much of the basic theory for which we use variables today, such as school geometry and algebra, was developed thousands of years ago, but the use of symbolic formulae and variables is only several hundreds of years old.

   a. 2-bridge knot
   b. -equivalence
   c. -module
   d. Variable

4. _____ is the mathematical process of putting things together. The plus sign '+' means that numbers are added together. For example, in the picture on the right, there are 3 + 2 apples--meaning three apples and two other apples--which is the same as five apples, since 3 + 2 = 5.
   a. AKS primality test
   b. Addition
   c. Abelian P-root group
   d. ADE classification

Chapter 3. Linear Inequalities and Absolute Value

5. In mathematics, an _____ is a statement about the relative size or order of two objects, or about whether they are the same or not

- The notation a < b means that a is less than b.
- The notation a > b means that a is greater than b.
- The notation a ≠ b means that a is not equal to b, but does not say that one is bigger than the other or even that they can be compared in size.

In all these cases, a is not equal to b, hence, '_____'.

These relations are known as strict _____

- The notation a ≤ b means that a is less than or equal to b (or, equivalently, not greater than b);
- The notation a ≥ b means that a is greater than or equal to b (or, equivalently, not smaller than b);

An additional use of the notation is to show that one quantity is much greater than another, normally by several orders of magnitude.

- The notation a ≪ b means that a is much less than b.
- The notation a ≫ b means that a is much greater than b.

If the sense of the _____ is the same for all values of the variables for which its members are defined, then the _____ is called an 'absolute' or 'unconditional' _____. If the sense of an _____ holds only for certain values of the variables involved, but is reversed or destroyed for other values of the variables, it is called a conditional _____.

One can apply the same algebraic operations to inequalities as one would apply for solving equalities. For example, to find x for the _____ 10x > 20 one would divide 20 by 10 to obtain x > 2.

a. AKS primality test
b. Abelian P-root group
c. ADE classification
d. Inequality

6. In mathematics, the word _____ is a term for any well-formed combination of mathematical symbols. For example,

$$x^2 + 3x - 4$$

is an _____, while

)x) / 0

is not, because the parentheses are not balanced and division by zero is undefined.

Chapter 3. Linear Inequalities and Absolute Value

Being an _____ is a syntactic concept - the meaning of the variables is irrelevant, but different fields have different notions of validity. See formal language for how expressions are constructed, and formal semantics for meaning.

   a. Orthogonal
   b. Unit ring
   c. Arity
   d. Expression

7. In mathematics, the _____ of two sets A and B is the set that contains all elements of A that also belong to B (or equivalently, all elements of B that also belong to A), but no other elements.

For explanation of the symbols used in this article, refer to the table of mathematical symbols.

The _____ of A and B

The _____ of A and B is written 'A ∩ B'.

   a. Abelian P-root group
   b. ADE classification
   c. AKS primality test
   d. Intersection

8. In its simplest meaning in mathematics and logic, an _____ is an action or procedure which produces a new value from one or more input values. There are two common types of operations: unary and binary. Unary operations involve only one value, such as negation and trigonometric functions.
   a. AKS primality test
   b. ADE classification
   c. Abelian P-root group
   d. Operation

9. In set theory, the term _____ refers to a set operation used in the convergence of set elements to form a resultant set containing the elements of both sets. As a simple example, a _____ of two disjoint sets, which do not have elements in common results in a set containing all elements from both sets. A Venn diagram representing the _____ of sets A and B. If one circle represents A, and the other B, then the red area represents the _____ of A and B. The area where the circles join, also shown in red, is the intersection of the two sets.

Chapter 3. Linear Inequalities and Absolute Value

If we define two sets which contain unique elements; those of A not occurring in B and vice versa, then the _____ of these sets results in a set which contains all elements of A and B. In terms of notation, we could define this set operation as the following:

A = {1,2,3,4}
B = {5,6,7,8}
$$A \cup B = \{1, 2, 3, 4, 5, 6, 7, 8\}$$

Other more complex operations can be done including the _____, if the set is for example defined by a property rather than a finite or assumed infinite enumeration of elements.

a. AKS primality test
b. ADE classification
c. Union
d. Abelian P-root group

Chapter 4. Graphs, Linear Equations, and Functions

1. In mathematics, a _____ in a (unital) ring R is an invertible element of R, i.e. an element u such that there is a v in R with

    uv = vu = 1_R, where 1_R is the multiplicative identity element.

    That is, u is an invertible element of the multiplicative monoid of R. If $0 \neq 1$ in the ring, then 0 is not a _____.

    Unfortunately, the term _____ is also used to refer to the identity element 1_R of the ring, in expressions like ring with a _____ or _____ ring, and also e.g. '_____' matrix.

    a. Ore extension
    b. Unit
    c. Ore condition
    d. Ascending chain condition on principal ideals

2. In mathematics, in the field of group theory, a _____ of a finite group is a quasisimple subnormal subgroup. Any two distinct components commute. The product of all the components is the layer of the group.
    a. Group homomorphism
    b. Stallings' theorem about ends of groups
    c. Wreath product
    d. Component

3. In mathematics, a (B, N) _____ is a structure on groups of Lie type that allows one to give uniform proofs of many results, instead of giving a large number of case-by-case proofs. Roughly speaking, it shows that all such groups are similar to the general linear group over a field. They were invented by the mathematician Jacques Tits, and are also sometimes known as Tits systems.
    a. Rank of a group
    b. Pair
    c. Group representations
    d. Group action

4. In mathematics, a _____ is a flat surface. Planes can arise as subspaces of some higher dimensional space, as with the walls of a room, or they may enjoy an independent existence in their own right, as in the setting of Euclidean geometry

Chapter 4. Graphs, Linear Equations, and Functions

a. -equivalence
b. Similarity
c. Plane
d. -module

5. In mathematics, the _____ of a real number is its numerical value without regard to its sign. So, for example, 3 is the _____ of both 3 and −3.

The _____ of a number a is denoted by | a |.

a. Absolute value
b. Abelian P-root group
c. ADE classification
d. AKS primality test

6. In geometry, a _____ is a straight curve. When geometry is used to model the real world, lines are used to represent straight objects with negligible width and height. Lines are an idealisation of such objects and have no width or height at all and are usually considered to be infinitely long.

a. 2-bridge knot
b. -module
c. -equivalence
d. Line

7. A _____ is a symbol that stands for a value that may vary; the term usually occurs in opposition to constant, which is a symbol for a non-varying value, i.e. completely fixed or fixed in the context of use. The concepts of constants and variables are fundamental to all modern mathematics, science, engineering, and computer programming.

Much of the basic theory for which we use variables today, such as school geometry and algebra, was developed thousands of years ago, but the use of symbolic formulae and variables is only several hundreds of years old.

a. -equivalence
b. -module
c. 2-bridge knot
d. Variable

8. In mathematics, the complex numbers are an extension of the real numbers obtained by adjoining an imaginary unit, denoted i, which satisfies:

Chapter 4. Graphs, Linear Equations, and Functions

$$i^2 = -1.$$

Every _____ can be written in the form a + bi, where a and b are real numbers called the real part and the imaginary part of the _____, respectively.

Complex numbers are a field, and thus have addition, subtraction, multiplication, and division operations. These operations extend the corresponding operations on real numbers, although with a number of additional elegant and useful properties, e.g., negative real numbers can be obtained by squaring complex (imaginary) numbers.

  a. -module
  b. Complex number
  c. 2-bridge knot
  d. -equivalence

9. In mathematics, an _____ is the finite or bounded case of a conic section, the geometric shape that results from cutting a circular conical or cylindrical surface with an oblique plane . It is also the locus of all points of the plane whose distances to two fixed points add to the same constant.

Ellipses also arise as images of a circle or a sphere under parallel projection, and some cases of perspective projection.

  a. ADE classification
  b. Ellipse
  c. AKS primality test
  d. Abelian P-root group

10. In geometry, a _____ is a part of a line that is bounded by two end points, and contains every point on the line between its end points. Examples of line segments include the sides of a triangle or square. More generally, when the end points are both vertices of a polygon, the _____ is either an edge (of that polygon) if they are adjacent vertices, or otherwise a diagonal.
  a. -module
  b. -equivalence
  c. Line segment
  d. Skew lines

11. In geometry, two lines or planes (or a line and a plane), are considered _____ to each other if they form congruent adjacent angles (an L-shape.) The term may be used as a noun or adjective. Thus, referring to Figure 1, the line AB is the _____ to CD through the point B. Note that by definition, a line is infinitely long, and strictly speaking AB and CD in this example represent line segments of two infinitely long lines.
    a. -equivalence
    b. -module
    c. 2-bridge knot
    d. Perpendicular

12. In mathematics, the word _____ is a term for any well-formed combination of mathematical symbols. For example,

    $x^2 + 3x - 4$

is an _____, while

    $)x) / 0$

is not, because the parentheses are not balanced and division by zero is undefined.

Being an _____ is a syntactic concept - the meaning of the variables is irrelevant, but different fields have different notions of validity.â€See formal language for how expressions are constructed, and formal semantics for meaning.

   a. Unit ring
   b. Expression
   c. Arity
   d. Orthogonal

13. In mathematics, the _____ of two sets A and B is the set that contains all elements of A that also belong to B (or equivalently, all elements of B that also belong to A), but no other elements.

For explanation of the symbols used in this article, refer to the table of mathematical symbols.

The _____ of A and B

The _____ of A and B is written 'A ∩ B'.

a. Intersection
b. ADE classification
c. Abelian P-root group
d. AKS primality test

14. In set theory, the term _____ refers to a set operation used in the convergence of set elements to form a resultant set containing the elements of both sets. As a simple example, a _____ of two disjoint sets, which do not have elements in common results in a set containing all elements from both sets. A Venn diagram representing the _____ of sets A and B. If one circle represents A, and the other B, then the red area represents the _____ of A and B. The area where the circles join, also shown in red, is the intersection of the two sets.

If we define two sets which contain unique elements; those of A not occurring in B and vice versa, then the _____ of these sets results in a set which contains all elements of A and B. In terms of notation, we could define this set operation as the following:

A = {1,2,3,4}
B = {5,6,7,8}
$$A \cup B = \{1, 2, 3, 4, 5, 6, 7, 8\}$$

Other more complex operations can be done including the _____, if the set is for example defined by a property rather than a finite or assumed infinite enumeration of elements.

a. ADE classification
b. AKS primality test
c. Abelian P-root group
d. Union

15. In mathematics, especially in the area of abstract algebra known as ring theory, a _____ is a ring with $0 \neq 1$ such that ab = 0 implies that either a = 0 or b = 0 (the zero-product property.) That is, it is a nontrivial ring without left or right zero divisors. A commutative _____ is called an integral _____.
a. Coherent ring
b. Subring
c. Partially-ordered ring
d. Domain

16. In mathematics, a _____ is any function which can be written as the ratio of two polynomial functions. _____ of degree 2 : $y = \dfrac{x^2 - 3x - 2}{x^2 - 4}$

In the case of one variable, x, a _____ is a function of the form

$$f(x) = \frac{P(x)}{Q(x)}$$

where P and Q are polynomial function in x and Q is not the zero polynomial. The domain of f is the set of all points x for which the denominator Q(x) is not zero.

a. Legendre rational functions
b. -equivalence
c. -module
d. Rational function

Chapter 5. Systems of Linear Equations

1. In mathematics, a _____ is a collection of linear equations involving the same set of variables. For example,

$$3x + 2y - z = 1$$
$$2x - 2y + 4z = -2$$
$$-x + \tfrac{1}{2}y - z = 0$$

is a system of three equations in the three variables x, y, z. A solution to a linear system is an assignment of numbers to the variables such that all the equations are simultaneously satisfied.

   a. -equivalence
   b. -module
   c. Simultaneous equations
   d. System of linear equations

2. A _____ is a symbol that stands for a value that may vary; the term usually occurs in opposition to constant, which is a symbol for a non-varying value, i.e. completely fixed or fixed in the context of use. The concepts of constants and variables are fundamental to all modern mathematics, science, engineering, and computer programming.

   Much of the basic theory for which we use variables today, such as school geometry and algebra, was developed thousands of years ago, but the use of symbolic formulae and variables is only several hundreds of years old.

   a. Variable
   b. 2-bridge knot
   c. -equivalence
   d. -module

3. An _____ is an equation in a system of simultaneous equations which cannot be derived algebraically from the other equations.
   a. Elementary matrix
   b. Orthogonalization
   c. Independent equation
   d. Eigendecomposition

4. In geometry, a _____ is a straight curve. When geometry is used to model the real world, lines are used to represent straight objects with negligible width and height. Lines are an idealisation of such objects and have no width or height at all and are usually considered to be infinitely long.

a. -module
   b. Line
   c. 2-bridge knot
   d. -equivalence

5. In mathematics, the _____ of a real number is its numerical value without regard to its sign. So, for example, 3 is the _____ of both 3 and −3.

The _____ of a number a is denoted by $|a|$.

   a. Absolute value
   b. AKS primality test
   c. Abelian P-root group
   d. ADE classification

6. In linear algebra, the _____ of a matrix is obtained by changing a matrix in some way.

Given the matrices A and B, where:

$$A = \begin{bmatrix} 1 & 3 & 2 \\ 2 & 0 & 1 \\ 5 & 2 & 2 \end{bmatrix}, \quad B = \begin{bmatrix} 4 \\ 3 \\ 1 \end{bmatrix}$$

Then, the _____ is written as:

$$(A|B) = \begin{bmatrix} 1 & 3 & 2 & 4 \\ 2 & 0 & 1 & 3 \\ 5 & 2 & 2 & 1 \end{bmatrix}$$

This is useful when solving systems of linear equations or the _____ may also be used to find the inverse of a matrix by combining it with the identity matrix.

$$C = \begin{bmatrix} 1 & 3 \\ -5 & 0 \end{bmatrix}$$

Let C be a square 2×2 matrix where

To find the inverse of C we create (C|I) where I is the 2×2 identity matrix.

Chapter 5. Systems of Linear Equations

a. Euclidean distance matrix
b. Unistochastic matrix
c. Unitary matrix
d. Augmented matrix

7. In mathematics, a _____ is a rectangular array of numbers. This way, matrices can record data that depend on multiple parameters. In particular they are used to keep track of the coefficients of multiple linear equations. Matrices are closely connected to linear transformations, which are higher-dimensional analogs of linear functions, i.e., functions of the form f(x) = c · x, where c is a constant. This map corresponds to a _____ with one row and column, with entry c. In addition to a number of elementary, entrywise operations such as _____ addition a key notion is _____ multiplication, which displays a number of features not encountered in numbers; for example, products of matrices depend on the order of the factors, unlike products of real numbers, say, where c · d = d · c for any two numbers c and d.

a. Polynomial expression
b. Matrix
c. Commutativity
d. Heap

8. In linear algebra a matrix is in _____ if

- All nonzero rows are above any rows of all zeroes, and
- The leading coefficient (also called pivot) of a row is always strictly to the right of the leading coefficient of the row above it.

Some texts add a third condition:

- The leading coefficient of each nonzero row is one.

A matrix is in reduced _____ if it satisfies the above three conditions, and if, in addition

- Every leading coefficient is 1 and is the only nonzero entry in its column.

The first non-zero entry in each row is called a pivot.

This matrix is in reduced _____:

$$\begin{bmatrix} 1 & 0 & 0 & 0 & 0 \\ 0 & 1 & 0 & 0 & 0 \\ 0 & 0 & 1 & 0 & 0 \\ 0 & 0 & 0 & 1 & 0 \end{bmatrix}$$

Chapter 5. Systems of Linear Equations 25

The following matrix is also in _____, but not in reduced row form:

$$\begin{bmatrix} 1 & 9 & 1 & 1 \\ 0 & 1 & 0 & 2 \\ 0 & 0 & 1 & 3 \end{bmatrix}$$

However, this matrix is not in _____, as the leading coefficient of row 3 is not strictly to the right of the leading coefficient of row 2, and the main diagonal is not made up of only ones.

$$\begin{bmatrix} 1 & 2 & 3 & 4 \\ 0 & 3 & 7 & 2 \\ 0 & 2 & 0 & 0 \end{bmatrix}$$

Every non-zero matrix can be reduced to an infinite number of echelon forms (they can all be multiples of each other, for example) via elementary matrix transformations.

a. -equivalence
b. 2-bridge knot
c. -module
d. Row echelon form

9. In its simplest meaning in mathematics and logic, an _____ is an action or procedure which produces a new value from one or more input values. There are two common types of operations: unary and binary. Unary operations involve only one value, such as negation and trigonometric functions.
a. Abelian P-root group
b. AKS primality test
c. ADE classification
d. Operation

Chapter 6. Exponents and Polynomials

1. In mathematics, the word _____ is a term for any well-formed combination of mathematical symbols. For example,

    $x^2 + 3x - 4$

    is an _____, while

    $)x) / 0$

    is not, because the parentheses are not balanced and division by zero is undefined.

    Being an _____ is a syntactic concept - the meaning of the variables is irrelevant, but different fields have different notions of validity.â€¢See formal language for how expressions are constructed, and formal semantics for meaning.

    a. Unit ring
    b. Arity
    c. Orthogonal
    d. Expression

2. The _____ are natural numbers including 0 ' href='/wiki/0_(number)'>0, 1, 2, 3, ...) and their negatives (0, −1, −2, −3, ...). They are numbers that can be written without a fractional or decimal component, and fall within the set {...
    a. Abelian P-root group
    b. AKS primality test
    c. ADE classification
    d. Integers

3. The _____ of a Lie algebra $\mathfrak{g}$ is a particular ideal of $\mathfrak{g}$.

    Let $\mathfrak{g}$ be a Lie algebra. The _____ of $\mathfrak{g}$ is defined as the largest solvable ideal of $\mathfrak{g}$.

    a. Class sum
    b. Garside element
    c. Radical
    d. Cyclically reduced word

4. In mathematics, there are several meanings of _____ depending on the subject.

    A _____, usually denoted by ° (the _____ symbol), is a measurement of plane angle, representing $\frac{1}{360}$ of a full rotation. When that angle is with respect to a reference meridian, it indicates a location along a great circle of a sphere, such as Earth, Mars, or the celestial sphere.

Chapter 6. Exponents and Polynomials

a. Relation algebra
b. Median algebra
c. Symmetric difference
d. Degree

5. _____ is the mathematical process of putting things together. The plus sign '+' means that numbers are added together. For example, in the picture on the right, there are 3 + 2 apples--meaning three apples and two other apples--which is the same as five apples, since 3 + 2 = 5.
   a. ADE classification
   b. Addition
   c. Abelian P-root group
   d. AKS primality test

6. In elementary algebra, a _____ is a polynomial with two terms--the sum of two monomials--often bound by parenthesis or brackets when operated upon. It is the simplest kind of polynomial other than monomials.

   - The _____ $a^2 - b^2$ can be factored as the product of two other binomials:

     $a^2 - b^2 = (a + b)(a - b.)$

     This is a special case of the more general formula: $a^{n+1} - b^{n+1} = (a-b)\sum_{k=0}^{n} a^k b^{n-k}$.

   - The product of a pair of linear binomials (ax + b) and (cx + d) is:

     $(ax + b)(cx + d) = acx^2 + axd + bcx + bd.$

   - A _____ raised to the nth power, represented as

     $(a + b)^n$

     can be expanded by means of the _____ theorem or, equivalently, using Pascal's triangle. Taking a simple example, the perfect square _____ $(p + q)^2$ can be found by squaring the :first digit, adding twice the product of the first and second digit and finally adding the square of the second digit, to give $p^2 + 2pq + q^2$.

a. Generalized arithmetic progression
b. Content
c. Theory of equations
d. Binomial

Chapter 6. Exponents and Polynomials

7. When a polynomial is expressed as a sum or difference of terms (e.g., in standard or canonical form), the exponent of the term with the highest exponent is the _____. The degree of a term is the sum of the powers of each variable in the term. The words degree and order are used interchangeably.
    a. Lommel polynomial
    b. Degree of the polynomial
    c. Multivariate division algorithm
    d. Secondary polynomials

8. In mathematics, the word _____ means two different things in the context of polynomials:

    - The first meaning is a product of powers of variables, or formally any value obtained from 1 by finitely many multiplications by a variable. If only a single variable x is considered this means that any _____ is either 1 or a power x^n of x, with n a positive integer. If several variables are considered, say, x, y, z, then each can be given an exponent, so that any _____ is of the form $x^a y^b z^c$ with a,b,c nonnegative integers (taking note that any exponent 0 makes the corresponding factor equal to 1.)
    - The second meaning of _____ includes monomials in the first sense, but also allows multiplication by any constant, so that − $7x^5$ and $(3 - 4i)x^4 yz^{13}$ are also considered to be monomials (the second example assuming polynomials in x, y, z over the complex numbers are considered.)

With either definition, the set of monomials is a subset of all polynomials that is closed under multiplication.

Both uses of this notion can be found, and in many cases the distinction is simply ignored, see for instance examples for the first and second meaning, and an unclear definition. In informal discussions the distinction is seldom important, and tendency is towards the broader second meaning. When studying the structure of polynomials however, one often definitely needs a notion with the first meaning.

    a. Schur polynomials
    b. Diagonal form
    c. Power sum symmetric polynomial
    d. Monomial

9. In elementary algebra, a _____ is a polynomial consisting of three terms; in other words, a _____ is the sum of three monomials. It can be factored using simple steps.

In linguistics, a _____ is a fixed expression which is made from three words; e.g. 'lights, camera, action', 'signed, sealed, delivered'.

Chapter 6. Exponents and Polynomials

a. Finitary operation
b. Polynomial Diophantine equation
c. Trinomial
d. Hall polynomials

10. _____ is one of the four basic arithmetic operations; it is the inverse of addition, meaning that if we start with any number and add any number and then subtract the same number we added, we return to the number we started with. _____ is denoted by a minus sign in infix notation.

The traditional names for the parts of the formula

   c − b = a

are minuend (c) − subtrahend (b) = difference (a.)

a. 2-bridge knot
b. Subtraction
c. -equivalence
d. -module

11. In mathematics, the complex numbers are an extension of the real numbers obtained by adjoining an imaginary unit, denoted i, which satisfies:

$$i^2 = -1.$$

Every _____ can be written in the form a + bi, where a and b are real numbers called the real part and the imaginary part of the _____, respectively.

Complex numbers are a field, and thus have addition, subtraction, multiplication, and division operations. These operations extend the corresponding operations on real numbers, although with a number of additional elegant and useful properties, e.g., negative real numbers can be obtained by squaring complex (imaginary) numbers.

a. 2-bridge knot
b. -equivalence
c. -module
d. Complex number

12. In its simplest meaning in mathematics and logic, an _____ is an action or procedure which produces a new value from one or more input values. There are two common types of operations: unary and binary. Unary operations involve only one value, such as negation and trigonometric functions.

   a. Operation
   b. AKS primality test
   c. ADE classification
   d. Abelian P-root group

13. In mathematics, the _____ of a real number is its numerical value without regard to its sign. So, for example, 3 is the _____ of both 3 and −3.

The _____ of a number a is denoted by $|a|$.

   a. Abelian P-root group
   b. AKS primality test
   c. Absolute value
   d. ADE classification

14. In mathematics, the _____ is a conic section, the intersection of a right circular conical surface and a plane parallel to a generating straight line of that surface. Given a point (the focus) and a line (the directrix) that lie in a plane, the locus of points in that plane that are equidistant to them is a _____.

A particular case arises when the plane is tangent to the conical surface of a circle.

   a. -equivalence
   b. Parabola
   c. 2-bridge knot
   d. -module

15. In mathematics, especially in elementary arithmetic, _____ is an arithmetic operation which is the inverse of multiplication.

Specifically, if c times b equals a, written:

$$c \times b = a$$

where b is not zero, then a divided by b equals c, written:

$$\frac{a}{b} = c$$

For instance,

$$\frac{6}{3} = 2$$

since

$$2 \times 3 = 6.$$

In the above expression, a is called the dividend, b the divisor and c the quotient.

a. 2-bridge knot
b. -equivalence
c. -module
d. Division

16. The _____ in algebra is an application of polynomial long division. It states that the remainder, r, of a polynomial, $f(x)$, divided by a linear divisor, $x - a$, is equal to $f(a)$.

This follows from the definition of polynomial long division; denoting the divisor, quotient and remainder by, respectively, $g(x)$, $q(x)$, and $r(x)$, polynomial long division gives a solution of the equation

$$f(x) = q(x)g(x) + r(x),$$

where the degree of $r(x)$ is less than that of $g(x)$.

If we take $g(x) = x - a$ as the divisor, giving the degree of $r(x)$ as 0, i.e. $r(x) = r$:

$$f(x) = q(x)(x - a) + r.$$

Setting $x = a$ we obtain:

$$f(a) = r.$$

Chapter 6. Exponents and Polynomials

The _____ may be used to evaluate $f(a)$ by calculating the remainder, r.

a. Ring of symmetric functions
b. Littlewood polynomial
c. Polynomial remainder theorem
d. Lommel polynomial

17. A _____ is a three-dimensional solid object bounded by six square faces, facets or sides, with three meeting at each vertex. The _____ can also be called a regular hexahedron and is one of the five Platonic solids. It is a special kind of square prism, of rectangular parallelepiped and of trigonal trapezohedron.

a. -module
b. 2-bridge knot
c. -equivalence
d. Cube

18. In mathematics, _____(F_n) is the outer automorphism group of a free group on n generators. These groups play an important role in geometric group theory.

_____(F_n) acts geometrically on a cell complex known as outer space, which can be thought of as the Teichmüller space for a bouquet of circles.

a. AKS primality test
b. Out
c. Abelian P-root group
d. ADE classification

19. In mathematics, the _____ is when a number is squared and is then subtracted from another squared number. It refers to the identity

$$a^2 - b^2 = (a+b)(a-b)$$

from elementary algebra.

The proof is straightforward, starting from the RHS: apply the distributive law to get a sum of four terms, and set

$$ba - ab = 0$$

as an application of the commutative law.

a. Cubic function
b. FOIL rule
c. Pointwise product
d. Difference of two squares

20. In mathematics, a _____ is a polynomial equation of the second degree. The general form is

$$ax^2 + bx + c = 0$$

The quadratic coefficient a is the coefficient of x^2, the linear coefficient b is the coefficient of x, and c is the constant coefficient, also called the free term or constant term.

Quadratic equations are called quadratic because the variable in the leading term is squared.

a. Cubic function
b. Quadratic equation
c. Rationalisation
d. Difference of two squares

21. In geometry, a _____ is a straight curve. When geometry is used to model the real world, lines are used to represent straight objects with negligible width and height. Lines are an idealisation of such objects and have no width or height at all and are usually considered to be infinitely long.
a. -module
b. Line
c. 2-bridge knot
d. -equivalence

22. A _____, in mathematics, is a polynomial function of the form f(x) = ax² + bx + c = 0, where $a \neq 0$. The graph of a _____ is a parabola whose major axis is parallel to the y-axis.

The expression ax² + bx + c in the definition of a _____ is a polynomial of degree 2 or second order, or a 2nd degree polynomial, because the highest exponent of x is 2.

a. Factor theorem
b. Dickson polynomials
c. Quadratic function
d. Vandermonde polynomial

Chapter 7. Rational Expressions

1. In mathematics, especially in the area of abstract algebra known as ring theory, a _____ is a ring with 0 ≠ 1 such that ab = 0 implies that either a = 0 or b = 0 (the zero-product property.) That is, it is a nontrivial ring without left or right zero divisors. A commutative _____ is called an integral _____.

    a. Partially-ordered ring
    b. Subring
    c. Domain
    d. Coherent ring

2. In mathematics, the word _____ is a term for any well-formed combination of mathematical symbols. For example,

    $x^2 + 3x - 4$

    is an _____, while

)x) / 0

    is not, because the parentheses are not balanced and division by zero is undefined.

    Being an _____ is a syntactic concept - the meaning of the variables is irrelevant, but different fields have different notions of validity.â€€See formal language for how expressions are constructed, and formal semantics for meaning.

    a. Expression
    b. Arity
    c. Orthogonal
    d. Unit ring

3. In mathematics, a _____ is any function which can be written as the ratio of two polynomial functions. _____ of degree 2 : $$y = \frac{x^2 - 3x - 2}{x^2 - 4}$$

    In the case of one variable, x, a _____ is a function of the form

    $$f(x) = \frac{P(x)}{Q(x)}$$

    where P and Q are polynomial function in x and Q is not the zero polynomial. The domain of f is the set of all points x for which the denominator Q(x) is not zero.

Chapter 7. Rational Expressions

   a. Rational function
   b. -equivalence
   c. Legendre rational functions
   d. -module

4. In mathematics, a _____ of a number x is any number which, when repeatedly multiplied by itself, eventually yields x:

$$r \times r \times \cdots \times r = x.$$

In terms of exponentiation, r is a _____ of x if

$$r^n = x$$

for some positive integer n. For example, 2 is a _____ of 16 since $2^4 = 2 \times 2 \times 2 \times 2 = 16$.

The number n is called the degree of the _____.

   a. Difference of two squares
   b. Rationalisation
   c. Root
   d. Cubic function

5. In mathematics, a _____ is any number that can be expressed in the form

$$\frac{a}{b}, a, b \in \mathbb{Z}, b \neq 0$$

which says 'a divided by b, given that a and b are integers and b does not equal zero'. Since the denominator b may be equal to 1, every integer is a _____. The set of all rational numbers is denoted $\mathbb{Q}$ (for quotient.)

   a. -equivalence
   b. Ratio
   c. Rational number
   d. Number system

6. In mathematics, especially in elementary arithmetic, _____ is an arithmetic operation which is the inverse of multiplication.

Specifically, if c times b equals a, written:

$$c \times b = a$$

where b is not zero, then a divided by b equals c, written:

$$\frac{a}{b} = c$$

For instance,

$$\frac{6}{3} = 2$$

since

$$2 \times 3 = 6.$$

In the above expression, a is called the dividend, b the divisor and c the quotient.

   a. -equivalence
   b. -module
   c. 2-bridge knot
   d. Division

7. In mathematics, the complex numbers are an extension of the real numbers obtained by adjoining an imaginary unit, denoted i, which satisfies:

$$i^2 = -1.$$

Every _____ can be written in the form a + bi, where a and b are real numbers called the real part and the imaginary part of the _____, respectively.

Complex numbers are a field, and thus have addition, subtraction, multiplication, and division operations. These operations extend the corresponding operations on real numbers, although with a number of additional elegant and useful properties, e.g., negative real numbers can be obtained by squaring complex (imaginary) numbers.

a. -module
b. 2-bridge knot
c. -equivalence
d. Complex number

8. _____ is the mathematical process of putting things together. The plus sign '+' means that numbers are added together. For example, in the picture on the right, there are 3 + 2 apples--meaning three apples and two other apples--which is the same as five apples, since 3 + 2 = 5.
   a. Addition
   b. AKS primality test
   c. Abelian P-root group
   d. ADE classification

9. _____ is one of the four basic arithmetic operations; it is the inverse of addition, meaning that if we start with any number and add any number and then subtract the same number we added, we return to the number we started with. _____ is denoted by a minus sign in infix notation.

The traditional names for the parts of the formula

   c − b = a

are minuend (c) − subtrahend (b) = difference (a.)

   a. -module
   b. 2-bridge knot
   c. -equivalence
   d. Subtraction

10. In mathematics, there are several meanings of _____ depending on the subject.

A _____, usually denoted by ° (the _____ symbol), is a measurement of plane angle, representing $\frac{1}{360}$ of a full rotation. When that angle is with respect to a reference meridian, it indicates a location along a great circle of a sphere, such as Earth, Mars, or the celestial sphere.

Chapter 7. Rational Expressions

   a. Degree
   b. Relation algebra
   c. Median algebra
   d. Symmetric difference

11. When a polynomial is expressed as a sum or difference of terms (e.g., in standard or canonical form), the exponent of the term with the highest exponent is the _____. The degree of a term is the sum of the powers of each variable in the term. The words degree and order are used interchangeably.
   a. Multivariate division algorithm
   b. Degree of the polynomial
   c. Secondary polynomials
   d. Lommel polynomial

12. In mathematics, the _____ of a real number is its numerical value without regard to its sign. So, for example, 3 is the _____ of both 3 and −3.

The _____ of a number a is denoted by $|a|$.

   a. ADE classification
   b. Abelian P-root group
   c. AKS primality test
   d. Absolute value

13. In geometry, a _____ is a straight curve. When geometry is used to model the real world, lines are used to represent straight objects with negligible width and height. Lines are an idealisation of such objects and have no width or height at all and are usually considered to be infinitely long.
   a. -module
   b. 2-bridge knot
   c. -equivalence
   d. Line

14. In its simplest meaning in mathematics and logic, an _____ is an action or procedure which produces a new value from one or more input values. There are two common types of operations: unary and binary. Unary operations involve only one value, such as negation and trigonometric functions.

a. AKS primality test
b. Operation
c. ADE classification
d. Abelian P-root group

15. In algebra, a commutative ring R is said to be _____ if any of the following equivalent conditions holds:

   1. The localization $R_\mathfrak{m}$ of R at $\mathfrak{m}$ is a valuation ring for every maximal ideal $\mathfrak{m}$ of R.
   2. For all ideals $\mathfrak{a}, \mathfrak{b}$, and $\mathfrak{c}$,

   $$\mathfrak{a} \cap (\mathfrak{b} + \mathfrak{c}) = (\mathfrak{a} \cap \mathfrak{b}) + (\mathfrak{a} \cap \mathfrak{c})$$

   - For all ideals $\mathfrak{a}, \mathfrak{b}$, and $\mathfrak{c}$,

   $$\mathfrak{a} + (\mathfrak{b} \cap \mathfrak{c}) = (\mathfrak{a} + \mathfrak{b}) \cap (\mathfrak{a} + \mathfrak{c})$$

An _____ domain is called a Prüfer domain.

a. Exchange matrix
b. Inverse eigenvalues theorem
c. Ordered vector space
d. Arithmetical

16. In linear algebra, two n-by-n matrices A and B are called _____ if

$$B = P^{-1}AP$$

for some invertible n-by-n matrix P. _____ matrices represent the same linear transformation under two different bases, with P being the change of basis matrix.

The matrix P is sometimes called a similarity transformation. In the context of matrix groups, similarity is sometimes referred to as conjugacy, with _____ matrices being conjugate.

a. Zero matrix
b. Cartan matrix
c. Skew-symmetric
d. Similar

17. A _____ is one of the basic shapes of geometry: a polygon with three corners or vertices and three sides or edges which are line segments. A _____ with vertices A, B, and C is denoted ABC.

In Euclidean geometry any three non-collinear points determine a unique _____ and a unique plane (i.e. a two-dimensional Euclidean space.)

   a. -equivalence
   b. Triangle
   c. 2-bridge knot
   d. -module

Chapter 8. Roots and Radicals

1. A _____ is a three-dimensional solid object bounded by six square faces, facets or sides, with three meeting at each vertex. The _____ can also be called a regular hexahedron and is one of the five Platonic solids. It is a special kind of square prism, of rectangular parallelepiped and of trigonal trapezohedron.
    a. 2-bridge knot
    b. -module
    c. -equivalence
    d. Cube

2. In mathematics, a _____ of a number, denoted $\sqrt[3]{x}$ or $x^{1/3}$, is a number a such that $a^3 = x$. All real numbers have exactly one real _____ and a pair of complex conjugate roots, and all nonzero complex numbers have three distinct complex cube roots. For example, the real _____ of 8 is 2, because $2^3 = 8$.
    a. Cube root
    b. -module
    c. 2-bridge knot
    d. -equivalence

3. In mathematics, specifically group theory, the _____ of a subgroup H in a group G is the e;relative sizee; of H in G. For example, if H has _____ 2 in G, then intuitively e;halfe; of the elements of G lie in H. The _____ of H in G is usually denoted $|G : H|$ or $[G : H]$.

   If G and H are finite groups, then the _____ of H in G is simply the quotient of the orders of the two groups:

   $$|G : H| = \frac{|G|}{|H|}.$$

   By Lagrange's theorem, this number is always a positive integer.

   If G and H are infinite, then the _____ of H is G is defined as the number of cosets of H in G.

    a. Inner automorphism
    b. Even permutations
    c. Index
    d. Outer automorphism

Chapter 8. Roots and Radicals

4. In group theory, a branch of mathematics, the term _____ is used in two closely related senses:

   - the _____ of a group is its cardinality, i.e. the number of its elements;
   - the _____, sometimes period, of an element a of a group is the smallest positive integer m such that a^m = e (where e denotes the identity element of the group, and a^m denotes the product of m copies of a.) If no such m exists, we say that a has infinite _____. All elements of finite groups have finite _____.

We denote the _____ of a group G by ord(G) or $|G|$ and the _____ of an element a by ord(a) or $|a|$.

Example. The symmetric group S_3 has the following multiplication table.

This group has six elements, so ord(S_3) = 6.

   a. Index calculus algorithm
   b. Order
   c. Artin group
   d. Outer automorphism group

5. The _____ of a Lie algebra $\mathfrak{g}$ is a particular ideal of $\mathfrak{g}$.

Let $\mathfrak{g}$ be a Lie algebra. The _____ of $\mathfrak{g}$ is defined as the largest solvable ideal of $\mathfrak{g}$.

   a. Class sum
   b. Garside element
   c. Cyclically reduced word
   d. Radical

6. In mathematics, a _____ of a number x is any number which, when repeatedly multiplied by itself, eventually yields x:

$$r \times r \times \cdots \times r = x.$$

In terms of exponentiation, r is a _____ of x if

$$r^n = x$$

for some positive integer n. For example, 2 is a _____ of 16 since 2^4 = 2 × 2 × 2 × 2 = 16.

The number n is called the degree of the _____.

a. Cubic function
b. Root
c. Rationalisation
d. Difference of two squares

7. In mathematics, a _____ of a number x is a number r such that r² = x, or, in other words, a number r whose square (the result of multiplying the number by itself) is x.

Every non-negative real number x has a unique non-negative _____, called the principal _____, which is denoted with a radical symbol as $\sqrt{x}$, or, using exponent notation, as $x^{1/2}$. For example, the principal _____ of 9 is 3, denoted $\sqrt{9} = 3$, because 3² = 3 × 3 = 9.

a. -equivalence
b. -module
c. 2-bridge knot
d. Square root

8. In mathematics, the word _____ is a term for any well-formed combination of mathematical symbols. For example,

x² + 3x − 4

is an _____, while

)x) / 0

is not, because the parentheses are not balanced and division by zero is undefined.

Being an _____ is a syntactic concept - the meaning of the variables is irrelevant, but different fields have different notions of validity.â€¢See formal language for how expressions are constructed, and formal semantics for meaning.

a. Arity
b. Orthogonal
c. Unit ring
d. Expression

9. In mathematics, the _____ of a real number is its numerical value without regard to its sign. So, for example, 3 is the _____ of both 3 and −3.

The _____ of a number a is denoted by $|a|$.

a. Absolute value
b. Abelian P-root group
c. ADE classification
d. AKS primality test

10. In mathematics, a _____ is any number that can be expressed in the form

$$\frac{a}{b}, a, b \in \mathbb{Z}, b \neq 0$$

which says 'a divided by b, given that a and b are integers and b does not equal zero'. Since the denominator b may be equal to 1, every integer is a _____. The set of all rational numbers is denoted $\mathbb{Q}$ (for quotient.)

a. -equivalence
b. Rational number
c. Ratio
d. Number system

11. In mathematics, _____(F_n) is the outer automorphism group of a free group on n generators. These groups play an important role in geometric group theory.

_____(F_n) acts geometrically on a cell complex known as outer space, which can be thought of as the Teichmüller space for a bouquet of circles.

a. AKS primality test
b. Abelian P-root group
c. ADE classification
d. Out

12. In mathematics, especially in elementary arithmetic, _____ is an arithmetic operation which is the inverse of multiplication.

Specifically, if c times b equals a, written:

$$c \times b = a$$

where b is not zero, then a divided by b equals c, written:

$$\frac{a}{b} = c$$

For instance,

$$\frac{6}{3} = 2$$

since

$$2 \times 3 = 6.$$

In the above expression, a is called the dividend, b the divisor and c the quotient.

- a. 2-bridge knot
- b. -module
- c. -equivalence
- d. Division

13. In mathematics, the complex numbers are an extension of the real numbers obtained by adjoining an imaginary unit, denoted i, which satisfies:

$$i^2 = -1.$$

Every _____ can be written in the form a + bi, where a and b are real numbers called the real part and the imaginary part of the _____, respectively.

Complex numbers are a field, and thus have addition, subtraction, multiplication, and division operations. These operations extend the corresponding operations on real numbers, although with a number of additional elegant and useful properties, e.g., negative real numbers can be obtained by squaring complex (imaginary) numbers.

- a. -module
- b. -equivalence
- c. 2-bridge knot
- d. Complex number

14. A _____ is a triangle in which one angle is a right angle.

Chapter 8. Roots and Radicals

The side opposite the right angle is called the hypotenuse (side [BC] in the figure below.) In addition, the sides adjacent to the right angle are called legs or catheti (singular: cathetus.)

   a. Right triangle
   b. -module
   c. 2-bridge knot
   d. -equivalence

15. A _____ is one of the basic shapes of geometry: a polygon with three corners or vertices and three sides or edges which are line segments. A _____ with vertices A, B, and C is denoted ABC.

In Euclidean geometry any three non-collinear points determine a unique _____ and a unique plane (i.e. a two-dimensional Euclidean space.)

   a. -equivalence
   b. Triangle
   c. 2-bridge knot
   d. -module

16. _____ is the mathematical process of putting things together. The plus sign '+' means that numbers are added together. For example, in the picture on the right, there are 3 + 2 apples--meaning three apples and two other apples--which is the same as five apples, since 3 + 2 = 5.
   a. Abelian P-root group
   b. AKS primality test
   c. ADE classification
   d. Addition

17. _____ is one of the four basic arithmetic operations; it is the inverse of addition, meaning that if we start with any number and add any number and then subtract the same number we added, we return to the number we started with. _____ is denoted by a minus sign in infix notation.

The traditional names for the parts of the formula

   $c - b = a$

are minuend (c) − subtrahend (b) = difference (a.)

Chapter 8. Roots and Radicals

a. 2-bridge knot
b. -equivalence
c. Subtraction
d. -module

18. In elementary algebra, a _____ is a polynomial with two terms--the sum of two monomials--often bound by parenthesis or brackets when operated upon. It is the simplest kind of polynomial other than monomials.

- The _____ $a^2 - b^2$ can be factored as the product of two other binomials:

    $a^2 - b^2 = (a + b)(a - b.)$

    This is a special case of the more general formula:

    $$a^{n+1} - b^{n+1} = (a - b) \sum_{k=0}^{n} a^k b^{n-k}$$

- The product of a pair of linear binomials (ax + b) and (cx + d) is:

    $(ax + b)(cx + d) = acx^2 + axd + bcx + bd.$

- A _____ raised to the nth power, represented as

    $(a + b)^n$

    can be expanded by means of the _____ theorem or, equivalently, using Pascal's triangle. Taking a simple example, the perfect square _____ $(p + q)^2$ can be found by squaring the first digit, adding twice the product of the first and second digit and finally adding the square of the second digit, to give $p^2 + 2pq + q^2$.

a. Theory of equations
b. Content
c. Binomial
d. Generalized arithmetic progression

19. In mathematics, there are several meanings of _____ depending on the subject.

A _____, usually denoted by ° (the _____ symbol), is a measurement of plane angle, representing $\frac{1}{360}$ of a full rotation. When that angle is with respect to a reference meridian, it indicates a location along a great circle of a sphere, such as Earth, Mars, or the celestial sphere.

a. Median algebra
b. Degree
c. Relation algebra
d. Symmetric difference

20. When a polynomial is expressed as a sum or difference of terms (e.g., in standard or canonical form), the exponent of the term with the highest exponent is the _____. The degree of a term is the sum of the powers of each variable in the term. The words degree and order are used interchangeably.
   a. Multivariate division algorithm
   b. Lommel polynomial
   c. Secondary polynomials
   d. Degree of the polynomial

21. In algebra, a _____ of an element in a quadratic extension field of a field K is its image under the unique non-identity automorphism of the extended field that fixes K. If the extension is generated by a square root of an element r of K, then the _____ of $a + b\sqrt{r}$ is $a - b\sqrt{r}$ for $a, b \in K$, and in particular in the case of the field C of complex numbers as an extension of the field R of real numbers (where r = − 1), the complex _____ of a + bi is a − bi.

Forming the sum or product of any element of the extension field with its _____ always gives an element of K. This can be used to rewrite a quotient of numbers in the extended field so that the denominator lies in K, by multiplying numerator and denominator by the _____ of the denominator. This process is called rationalization of the denominator, in particular if K is the field Q of rational numbers.

   a. Conjugate
   b. Field arithmetic
   c. K-theory
   d. Digital root

22. In mathematics, an _____ represents a solution, such as that to an equation, that emerges from the process of solving the problem but is not a valid solution to the original problem. A missing solution is a solution that was a valid solution to the original problem, but disappeared during the process of solving the problem. Both are frequently the consequence of performing operations that are not invertible for some or all values of the variables, which disturbs the chain of logical implications in the proof.
   a. Unitary method
   b. Extraneous solution
   c. Equating the coefficients
   d. Unary operation

Chapter 8. Roots and Radicals

23. In geometry, a _____ is a straight curve. When geometry is used to model the real world, lines are used to represent straight objects with negligible width and height. Lines are an idealisation of such objects and have no width or height at all and are usually considered to be infinitely long.
    a. -equivalence
    b. -module
    c. 2-bridge knot
    d. Line

24. In mathematics, an _____ is a complex number whose squared value is a real number less than or equal to zero. The imaginary unit, denoted by i or j, is an example of an _____. If y is a real number, then i·y is an _____, because:

$$(i \cdot y)^2 = i^2 \cdot y^2 = -y^2 \leq 0.$$

Imaginary numbers were defined in 1572 by Rafael Bombelli.

   a. Abelian P-root group
   b. AKS primality test
   c. ADE classification
   d. Imaginary number

25. In its simplest meaning in mathematics and logic, an _____ is an action or procedure which produces a new value from one or more input values. There are two common types of operations: unary and binary. Unary operations involve only one value, such as negation and trigonometric functions.
    a. AKS primality test
    b. ADE classification
    c. Operation
    d. Abelian P-root group

Chapter 9. Quadratic Equations, Inequalities, and Graphs

1. In mathematics, a _____ is a polynomial equation of the second degree. The general form is

$$ax^2 + bx + c = 0$$

The quadratic coefficient a is the coefficient of x^2, the linear coefficient b is the coefficient of x, and c is the constant coefficient, also called the free term or constant term.

Quadratic equations are called quadratic because the variable in the leading term is squared.

   a. Rationalisation
   b. Quadratic equation
   c. Difference of two squares
   d. Cubic function

2. In mathematics, a _____ of a number x is a number r such that r^2 = x, or, in other words, a number r whose square (the result of multiplying the number by itself) is x.

Every non-negative real number x has a unique non-negative _____, called the principal _____, which is denoted with a radical symbol as $\sqrt{x}$, or, using exponent notation, as $x^{1/2}$. For example, the principal _____ of 9 is 3, denoted $\sqrt{9} = 3$, because 3^2 = 3 × 3 = 9.

   a. -equivalence
   b. -module
   c. Square root
   d. 2-bridge knot

3. In mathematics, the complex numbers are an extension of the real numbers obtained by adjoining an imaginary unit, denoted i, which satsfies:

$$i^2 = -1.$$

Every _____ can be written in the form a + bi, where a and b are real numbers called the real part and the imaginary part of the _____, respectively.

Complex numbers are a field, and thus have addition, subtraction, multiplication, and division operations. These operations extend the corresponding operations on real numbers, although with a number of additional elegant and useful properties, e.g., negative real numbers can be obtained by squaring complex (imaginary) numbers.

Chapter 9. Quadratic Equations, Inequalities, and Graphs

a. 2-bridge knot
b. -equivalence
c. -module
d. Complex number

4. In geometry, a _____ is a straight curve. When geometry is used to model the real world, lines are used to represent straight objects with negligible width and height. Lines are an idealisation of such objects and have no width or height at all and are usually considered to be infinitely long.

a. -module
b. -equivalence
c. Line
d. 2-bridge knot

5. In mathematics, a _____ of a number x is any number which, when repeatedly multiplied by itself, eventually yields x:

$$r \times r \times \cdots \times r = x.$$

In terms of exponentiation, r is a _____ of x if

$$r^n = x$$

for some positive integer n. For example, 2 is a _____ of 16 since $2^4 = 2 \times 2 \times 2 \times 2 = 16$.

The number n is called the degree of the _____.

a. Difference of two squares
b. Rationalisation
c. Cubic function
d. Root

6. In elementary algebra, _____ is a technique for converting a quadratic polynomial of the form

$$ax^2 + bx + c$$

Chapter 9. Quadratic Equations, Inequalities, and Graphs

to the form

$$a(\cdots\cdots)^2 + \text{constant}.$$

The expression inside the parenthesis is of the form x − constant. Thus one converts ax² + bx + c to

$$a(x-h)^2 + k$$

and one must find h and k.

_____ is used in

- solving quadratic equations,
- graphing quadratic functions,
- evaluating integrals in calculus,
- finding Laplace transforms.

In mathematics, _____ is considered a basic algebraic operation, and is often applied without remark in any computation involving quadratic polynomials.

There is a simple formula in elementary algebra for computing the square of a binomial:

$$(x+p)^2 = x^2 + 2px + p^2.$$

For example:

$$(x+3)^2 = x^2 + 6x + 9 \qquad (p=3)$$
$$(x-5)^2 = x^2 - 10x + 25 \qquad (p=-5).$$

In any perfect square, the number p is always half the coefficient of x, and then the constant term is equal to p².

a. Completing the square
b. Content
c. Nested radical
d. Reduct

7. In algebra, the _____ of a polynomial with real or complex coefficients is a certain expression in the coefficients of the polynomial which is a symmetric polynomial in the coefficients and gives information on the nature of the roots; in particular, it is equal to zero if and only if the polynomial has a multiple root (i.e. a root with multiplicity greater than one) in the complex numbers. For example, the _____ of the quadratic polynomial

$$ax^2 + bx + c \text{ is } b^2 - 4ac.$$

The _____ of the cubic polynomial

$$ax^3 + bx^2 + cx + d \text{ is } b^2c^2 - 4ac^3 - 4b^3d - 27a^2d^2 + 18abcd.$$

a. Discriminant
b. Polynomial remainder theorem
c. Kazhdan-Lusztig polynomials
d. Minimal polynomial

8. In mathematics, the word _____ is a term for any well-formed combination of mathematical symbols. For example,

$x^2 + 3x - 4$

is an _____, while

)x) / 0

is not, because the parentheses are not balanced and division by zero is undefined.

Being an _____ is a syntactic concept - the meaning of the variables is irrelevant, but different fields have different notions of validity.â€¢See formal language for how expressions are constructed, and formal semantics for meaning.

a. Arity
b. Orthogonal
c. Unit ring
d. Expression

9. A _____ is an expression which compares quantities relative to each other. The most common examples involve two quantities, but in theory any number of quantities can be compared. In mathematical terms, they are represented by separating each quantity with a colon, for example the _____ 2:3, which is read as the _____ 'two to three'.

a. -equivalence
b. Rational number
c. Number system
d. Ratio

10. A _____ is a triangle in which one angle is a right angle.

The side opposite the right angle is called the hypotenuse (side [BC] in the figure below.) In addition, the sides adjacent to the right angle are called legs or catheti (singular: cathetus.)

a. -module
b. Right triangle
c. -equivalence
d. 2-bridge knot

11. A _____ is one of the basic shapes of geometry: a polygon with three corners or vertices and three sides or edges which are line segments. A _____ with vertices A, B, and C is denoted ABC.

In Euclidean geometry any three non-collinear points determine a unique _____ and a unique plane (i.e. a two-dimensional Euclidean space.)

a. -module
b. -equivalence
c. 2-bridge knot
d. Triangle

12. A _____, in mathematics, is a polynomial function of the form f(x) = ax² + bx + c = 0, where $a \neq 0$. The graph of a _____ is a parabola whose major axis is parallel to the y-axis.

The expression ax² + bx + c in the definition of a _____ is a polynomial of degree 2 or second order, or a 2nd degree polynomial, because the highest exponent of x is 2.

a. Dickson polynomials
b. Quadratic function
c. Vandermonde polynomial
d. Factor theorem

Chapter 9. Quadratic Equations, Inequalities, and Graphs

13. In linear algebra, two n-by-n matrices A and B are called _____ if

$$B = P^{-1}AP$$

for some invertible n-by-n matrix P. _____ matrices represent the same linear transformation under two different bases, with P being the change of basis matrix.

The matrix P is sometimes called a similarity transformation. In the context of matrix groups, similarity is sometimes referred to as conjugacy, with _____ matrices being conjugate.

a. Skew-symmetric
b. Cartan matrix
c. Zero matrix
d. Similar

14. In mathematics, a _____ is a curve obtained by intersecting a cone (more precisely, a circular conical surface) with a plane. A _____ is therefore a restriction of a quadric surface to the plane. The conic sections were named and studied as long ago as 200 BC, when Apollonius of Perga undertook a systematic study of their properties.
a. Matrix representation of conic sections
b. Conic section
c. Derivation of the cartesian form for an ellipse
d. Dandelin spheres

15. In mathematics, the _____ is a conic section, the intersection of a right circular conical surface and a plane parallel to a generating straight line of that surface. Given a point (the focus) and a line (the directrix) that lie in a plane, the locus of points in that plane that are equidistant to them is a _____.

A particular case arises when the plane is tangent to the conical surface of a circle.

a. 2-bridge knot
b. -equivalence
c. -module
d. Parabola

16. In mathematics, the _____ of a real number is its numerical value without regard to its sign. So, for example, 3 is the _____ of both 3 and −3.

The _____ of a number a is denoted by $|a|$.

a. ADE classification
b. Absolute value
c. Abelian P-root group
d. AKS primality test

17.   In the mathematical field of topology, a _____ of a fiber bundle, π: E → B, over a topological space, B, is a continuous map, s : B → E, such that π(s(x))=x for all x in B.

A _____ is a certain generalization of the notion of the graph of a function. The graph of a function g : X → Y can be identified with a function taking its values in the Cartesian product E = X×Y of X and Y:

$$s(x) = (x, g(x)) \in E, \quad s : X \to E.$$

A _____ is an abstract characterization of what it means to be a graph.

a. Section
b. -module
c. Fiber bundle
d. -equivalence

Chapter 10. Exponential and Logarithmic Functions

1. In mathematics, a _____ is a collection of linear equations involving the same set of variables. For example,

$$3x + 2y - z = 1$$
$$2x - 2y + 4z = -2$$
$$-x + \tfrac{1}{2}y - z = 0$$

is a system of three equations in the three variables x, y, z. A solution to a linear system is an assignment of numbers to the variables such that all the equations are simultaneously satisfied.

   a. System of linear equations
   b. -module
   c. Simultaneous equations
   d. -equivalence

2. Any formula written in terms of logarithms may be said to be in _____.

In contexts including complex manifolds and algebraic geometry, a logarithmic differential form is a 1-form that, locally at least, can be written

$$\frac{df}{f}$$

for some meromorphic function (resp. rational function) f.

   a. Hankel contour
   b. Bispectrum
   c. Meromorphic function
   d. Logarithmic form

3. In mathematics, the _____ of a real number is its numerical value without regard to its sign. So, for example, 3 is the _____ of both 3 and −3.

The _____ of a number a is denoted by $|a|$.

   a. Absolute value
   b. ADE classification
   c. Abelian P-root group
   d. AKS primality test

Chapter 10. Exponential and Logarithmic Fundions

4. In mathematics, the word _____ is a term for any well-formed combination of mathematical symbols. For example,

   $x^2 + 3x - 4$

is an _____, while

)x) / 0

is not, because the parentheses are not balanced and division by zero is undefined.

Being an _____ is a syntactic concept - the meaning of the variables is irrelevant, but different fields have different notions of validity.â€¢See formal language for how expressions are constructed, and formal semantics for meaning.

   a. Arity
   b. Unit ring
   c. Orthogonal
   d. Expression

5. The _____ of a Lie algebra $\mathfrak{g}$ is a particular ideal of $\mathfrak{g}$.

Let $\mathfrak{g}$ be a Lie algebra. The _____ of $\mathfrak{g}$ is defined as the largest solvable ideal of $\mathfrak{g}$.

   a. Radical
   b. Class sum
   c. Garside element
   d. Cyclically reduced word

6. In geometry, two lines or planes (or a line and a plane), are considered _____ to each other if they form congruent adjacent angles (an L-shape.) The term may be used as a noun or adjective. Thus, referring to Figure 1, the line AB is the _____ to CD through the point B. Note that by definition, a line is infinitely long, and strictly speaking AB and CD in this example represent line segments of two infinitely long lines.
   a. 2-bridge knot
   b. -module
   c. -equivalence
   d. Perpendicular

7. In geometry, a _____ is a straight curve. When geometry is used to model the real world, lines are used to represent straight objects with negligible width and height. Lines are an idealisation of such objects and have no width or height at all and are usually considered to be infinitely long.
   a. 2-bridge knot
   b. -equivalence
   c. -module
   d. Line

Chapter 11. Nonlinear Fundions, Conic Sections, and Nonlinear Systems

1. In mathematics, a _____ is a curve obtained by intersecting a cone (more precisely, a circular conical surface) with a plane. A _____ is therefore a restriction of a quadric surface to the plane. The conic sections were named and studied as long ago as 200 BC, when Apollonius of Perga undertook a systematic study of their properties.

   a. Derivation of the cartesian form for an ellipse
   b. Matrix representation of conic sections
   c. Dandelin spheres
   d. Conic section

2. In mathematics, the _____ is a conic section, the intersection of a right circular conical surface and a plane parallel to a generating straight line of that surface. Given a point (the focus) and a line (the directrix) that lie in a plane, the locus of points in that plane that are equidistant to them is a _____.

   A particular case arises when the plane is tangent to the conical surface of a circle.

   a. -equivalence
   b. 2-bridge knot
   c. Parabola
   d. -module

3. In the mathematical field of topology, a _____ of a fiber bundle, π: E → B, over a topological space, B, is a continuous map, s : B → E, such that π(s(x))=x for all x in B.

   A _____ is a certain generalization of the notion of the graph of a function. The graph of a function g : X → Y can be identified with a function taking its values in the Cartesian product E = X×Y of X and Y:

   $$s(x) = (x, g(x)) \in E, \quad s : X \to E.$$

   A _____ is an abstract characterization of what it means to be a graph.

   a. -module
   b. -equivalence
   c. Fiber bundle
   d. Section

4. In mathematics, the _____ of a real number is its numerical value without regard to its sign. So, for example, 3 is the _____ of both 3 and −3.

   The _____ of a number a is denoted by $|a|$.

a. ADE classification
b. AKS primality test
c. Abelian P-root group
d. Absolute value

5. In mathematics, a _____ of a number x is a number r such that $r^2 = x$, or, in other words, a number r whose square (the result of multiplying the number by itself) is x.

Every non-negative real number x has a unique non-negative _____, called the principal _____, which is denoted with a radical symbol as $\sqrt{x}$, or, using exponent notation, as $x^{1/2}$. For example, the principal _____ of 9 is 3, denoted $\sqrt{9} = 3$, because $3^2 = 3 \times 3 = 9$.

a. -equivalence
b. Square root
c. -module
d. 2-bridge knot

6. In mathematics, a _____ of a number x is any number which, when repeatedly multiplied by itself, eventually yields x:

$$r \times r \times \cdots \times r = x.$$

In terms of exponentiation, r is a _____ of x if

$$r^n = x$$

for some positive integer n. For example, 2 is a _____ of 16 since $2^4 = 2 \times 2 \times 2 \times 2 = 16$.

The number n is called the degree of the _____.

a. Difference of two squares
b. Rationalisation
c. Root
d. Cubic function

7. In mathematics, a _____ represents the application of one function to the results of another. For instance, the functions f: X → Y and g: Y → Z can be composed by first computing f(x) and then applying a function g to the output of f(x.)

Thus one obtains a function g ∘ f: X → Z defined by (g ∘ f)(x) = g(f(x)) for all x in X. The notation g ∘ f is read as 'g circle f', or 'g composed with f', 'g after f', 'g following f', or just 'g of f'.

a. Reflection
b. Shear mappings
c. Linear map
d. Composite function

8. The term _____ or centre is used in various contexts in abstract algebra to denote the set of all those elements that commute with all other elements. More specifically:

- The _____ of a group G consists of all those elements x in G such that xg = gx for all g in G. This is a normal subgroup of G.
- The _____ of a ring R is the subset of R consisting of all those elements x of R such that xr = rx for all r in R. The _____ is a commutative subring of R, so R is an algebra over its _____.
- The _____ of an algebra A consists of all those elements x of A such that xa = ax for all a in A. See also: central simple algebra.
- The _____ of a Lie algebra L consists of all those elements x in L such that [x,a] = 0 for all a in L. This is an ideal of the Lie algebra L.
- The _____ of a monoidal category C consists of pairs (A,u) where A is an object of C, and $u: A \otimes - \to - \otimes A$ a natural isomorphism satisfying certain axioms.

a. Ring theory
b. Left alternative
c. Center
d. Self-adjoint

9. In mathematics, an _____ is the finite or bounded case of a conic section, the geometric shape that results from cutting a circular conical or cylindrical surface with an oblique plane . It is also the locus of all points of the plane whose distances to two fixed points add to the same constant.

Ellipses also arise as images of a circle or a sphere under parallel projection, and some cases of perspective projection.

a. Abelian P-root group
b. AKS primality test
c. ADE classification
d. Ellipse

10. In geometry, a _____ is a straight curve. When geometry is used to model the real world, lines are used to represent straight objects with negligible width and height. Lines are an idealisation of such objects and have no width or height at all and are usually considered to be infinitely long.
   a. Line
   b. -equivalence
   c. -module
   d. 2-bridge knot

11. In mathematics, the word _____ is a term for any well-formed combination of mathematical symbols. For example,

   $x^2 + 3x - 4$

is an _____, while

)x) / 0

is not, because the parentheses are not balanced and division by zero is undefined.

Being an _____ is a syntactic concept - the meaning of the variables is irrelevant, but different fields have different notions of validity.â€See formal language for how expressions are constructed, and formal semantics for meaning.

   a. Expression
   b. Unit ring
   c. Orthogonal
   d. Arity

12. In mathematics, an _____ is a statement about the relative size or order of two objects, or about whether they are the same or not

   - The notation a < b means that a is less than b.
   - The notation a > b means that a is greater than b.
   - The notation a ≠ b means that a is not equal to b, but does not say that one is bigger than the other or even that they can be compared in size.

In all these cases, a is not equal to b, hence, '_____'.

Chapter 11. Nonlinear Functions, Conic Sections, and Nonlinear Systems

These relations are known as strict _____

- The notation a ≤ b means that a is less than or equal to b (or, equivalently, not greater than b);
- The notation a ≥ b means that a is greater than or equal to b (or, equivalently, not smaller than b);

An additional use of the notation is to show that one quantity is much greater than another, normally by several orders of magnitude.

- The notation a ≪ b means that a is much less than b.
- The notation a ≫ b means that a is much greater than b.

If the sense of the _____ is the same for all values of the variables for which its members are defined, then the _____ is called an 'absolute' or 'unconditional' _____. If the sense of an _____ holds only for certain values of the variables involved, but is reversed or destroyed for other values of the variables, it is called a conditional _____.

One can apply the same algebraic operations to inequalities as one would apply for solving equalities. For example, to find x for the _____ 10x > 20 one would divide 20 by 10 to obtain x > 2.

a. Abelian P-root group
b. ADE classification
c. Inequality
d. AKS primality test

ANSWER KEY

Chapter 1
1. d   2. d   3. d   4. d   5. d   6. b   7. d   8. b   9. d   10. b
11. a   12. d   13. d   14. a   15. d   16. a   17. a   18. d   19. d   20. d
21. d   22. b   23. d   24. d   25. d   26. a

Chapter 2
1. b   2. d   3. d   4. d

Chapter 3
1. b   2. d   3. d   4. b   5. d   6. d   7. d   8. d   9. c

Chapter 4
1. b   2. d   3. b   4. c   5. a   6. d   7. d   8. b   9. b   10. c
11. d   12. b   13. a   14. d   15. d   16. d

Chapter 5
1. d   2. a   3. c   4. b   5. a   6. d   7. b   8. d   9. d

Chapter 6
1. d   2. d   3. c   4. d   5. b   6. d   7. b   8. d   9. c   10. b
11. d   12. a   13. c   14. b   15. d   16. c   17. d   18. b   19. d   20. b
21. b   22. c

Chapter 7
1. c   2. a   3. a   4. c   5. c   6. d   7. d   8. a   9. d   10. a
11. b   12. d   13. d   14. b   15. d   16. d   17. b

Chapter 8
1. d   2. a   3. c   4. b   5. d   6. b   7. d   8. d   9. a   10. b
11. d   12. d   13. d   14. a   15. b   16. d   17. c   18. c   19. b   20. d
21. a   22. b   23. d   24. d   25. c

Chapter 9
1. b   2. c   3. d   4. c   5. d   6. a   7. a   8. d   9. d   10. b
11. d   12. b   13. d   14. b   15. d   16. b   17. a

Chapter 10
1. a   2. d   3. a   4. d   5. a   6. d   7. d

Chapter 11
1. d   2. c   3. d   4. d   5. b   6. c   7. d   8. c   9. d   10. a
11. a   12. c

www.ingramcontent.com/pod-product-compliance
Lightning Source LLC
Chambersburg PA
CBHW081219230426
43666CB00015B/2802